Love
Poems

ALSO BY BRUCE B. WILMER

Feelings

Love
Poems

by Bruce B. Wilmer

Published and printed by:
Wilmer Graphics, Inc.
P. O. Box 140, Huntington, NY 11743

Certain poems in this book have been copyrighted individually in the form of graphic products, such as greeting cards, posters and scrolls, and/or in book form. The following are page references for these previously copyrighted poems arranged by copyright date. Those in bold print were included in an earlier general collection of 184 poems, published in 1987, entitled *FEELINGS*.

The following poems in this volume are being published for the first time:

Cover illustration and design: Beth Ann Beiter

Back cover photograph: Sydney Wilmer

Manufactured in the United States of America

First printing: December, 1990

(Edition) 1 2 3 4 5 6 7 8 9 10 — 95 94 93 92 91 90 (Year)

ISBN: 0-9615967-2-4

For Syd,
who gave my heart
a place to grow.

INTRODUCTION

LOVE POEMS is an affirmation of my twenty-four year love affair with the girl I married. However, it is a book about *love*, not marriage. It draws from my written feelings since 1976 and traces our partnership's past, present and future with affection and surprise. It also includes certain verses reflecting my empathy for other individuals and their relationships. This book is my proclamation that love need never grow old. Its new beginnings and rediscoveries give youth a constant perspective. Most importantly, it can be perfect when we're not. It stirs our sense of beauty and imagination, like a rainbow; it has the resilience of stone. It's our anchor to the universe, our place in time, our proof that we exist, our reason for existence.

This book is not a dissertation on love, just one person's grateful testimony and statement of wonder. Its pages compress fourteen years of feeling and plot the tender instants of time when love infused my spirit with warmth. As such, it is the pulse of my love, read over time. It is a tribute to the carefree, innocent and caring moments that have liberated my heart and pen. We all log special moments such as these now and again. With the patience of true conviction, I have attempted to record some of them. In so doing, I have given you a portrait of this poet's real source of inspiration, whose loving acceptance gave my heart a place to grow... *Love ya, Syd!*

Bruce B. Wilmer
December, 1990

CONTENTS

I'M GLAD I MET YOU

Our paths converged and softly touched—
    Our hearts moved close in greeting.
It was a time to sample change—
    It was a time for meeting.

An accident of chance became
    Our lasting gift that day.
Some paths may cross but do not always
    Join in such a way.

I'm glad you've shared your life with me
    And made this moment prime.
The future will preserve the warmth
    That fills this precious time.

The present is a prize
    That you have helped to make complete.
I'm glad that fate arranged a way
    For you and me to meet.

OUR LIVES TOUCHED

Love had but a little while,
    So love made me your friend.
The time thus spared, so briefly shared,
    Was all love had to lend.

I loved you for that moment
    When lives did briefly touch.
But in its way love wouldn't say
    How lasting or how much.

If life gives us another chance,
    We'll have the time to see
If love will have the patience
    To favor you and me.

But since we cannot hope to know
    Just what the future sends,
Let's value what we found together
    Knowing we were friends.

IF IT ONLY LASTS FOR NOW

If it only lasts for now,
    It's something special still.
If it is this moment's gift
    To cherish, then I will.

If it's but a fleeting flame
    We find in our today,
I know its tender message
    Will remain, not drift away.

If it is tomorrow's choice
    To say, let's now move on,
The memories within our hearts
    Won't fade and then be gone.

If it's only for today,
    This precious time let's claim;
For this is one pure moment
    When our hearts feel much the same.

BUT FOR CHANCE

But for chance, some paths don't cross,
    Some moments don't occur.
But for crystals formed in time,
    Some images just blur.

But for little accidents
    That turn our lives and change them,
Major forces wouldn't find
    Our dreams and rearrange them.

But for certain key events
    That interrupt our stride,
Worldly possibilities
    Would never seem so wide.

Losses, even setbacks,
    May propel our lives ahead.
Negatives may motivate
    And launch our goals instead.

Love may flourish, hopes may grow,
    And friendships may advance
Because of that imposing little
    Factor known as chance.

FIRST MEETING

I saw you across the room,
     Singled out of the group's lively conversing
As a solitary flower, sharply defined.

The blur of all else swirled around
     My heightened awareness of you,
Driving my evening toward the single objective
     Of meeting you amidst the confusion
          Of this chance encounter.

Words, now unremembered, consummated this
     Cosmic convergence of two lives,
This improbable crossing of paths
     Which drew our hearts from random orbit
          Into common trajectory.

What distant launch of spirit
     Could have programmed this moment
          So accurately.
What sudden transfusion of heart
     Implanted the moment forever
          In our shared consciousness.

This touch of time
     Could have been a near miss.
Our souls might have then roamed
     The vastness forever,
          Thwarted by fate,
Unaware that heaven had opened a crack
     And for one brief moment
          Let our mortal eyes
               View the possibility
                    Of each other.

WE HAD FUN TOGETHER

We had a lot of fun together,
  Got along so well,
That in my mind a host of rather
  Pleasant thoughts still dwell.

All the time we shared rushed by;
  Too soon our day had ended.
It's satisfying when two paths
  Have crossed and lives have blended.

There's so much more for us to learn,
  New thoughts we can exchange,
New feelings we can introduce,
  More sharing to arrange.

I hope you felt the same as I,
  Enjoyed the time completely.
It's hard for me to comprehend
  What all this means concretely.

But I just couldn't let
  This special moment disappear
Without informing you how much
  It meant to have you near.

I ENJOY BEING WITH YOU

I enjoy the time when I'm with you;
    I'm happy when we're talking.
I value all the things we do,
    The quiet moments walking.

So many things are better shared;
    And I'm so glad that we
Find such complete fulfillment in
    Each other's company.

There's more to life when you're around;
    You make me feel alive.
There's nothing I withhold from you;
    With you, my passions thrive.

I'm able to explore my thoughts,
    Relax in freedom found.
The confidence I feel is
    Reassuring and profound.

The moments we're together
    Are such special ones for me,
Because I sense that we exist
    In loving harmony.

I CARE FOR YOU

The moods of my mind
   Softly whisper and weave,
And the message I'm hearing
   Refuses to leave...
               I care for you.

In a world that is changing,
   As old patterns shift,
There's a recurrent meaning,
   A general drift...
               I care for you.

No incidents past
   Or memories now
Can silence the feelings
   That my thoughts allow...
               I care for you.

Relationships change
   And people do, too;
But a constant emotion
   Keeps filtering through...
               I care for you.

FINDING LOVE AGAIN

After life has lost its love
  And *now* erases *then*,
The lonely heart may choose the path
  Of finding love again.

The past will never fade and go
  Entirely away.
The beauty and the tragedy
  Are in the soul to stay.

But all that lives in memory
  Gives hope a new dimension.
A loss endured should not place love
  Forever in suspension.

The seasoned heart needs once again
  To feel a life of caring.
Two solitary lives can be
  Enriched through times of sharing.

Two hearts that look again for love
  Will find their passion strong.
Two lives that link in harmony
  Will sing a better song.

TWO FREE

My independence gives me freedom
    Only to be free;
But freedom tells me there is something
    I alone can't be.

For freedom's very private voice
    Must have a private hearing;
And selfless listening can't be found
    Without two people sharing.

Freedom's body, too, must find
    Through warmth its definition.
Alone its fires turn to cold
    Just wanting recognition.

And freedom's soul must find a match;
    New strength it must inherit.
If freedom grows, it's when it knows
    It's found a kindred spirit.

I'LL WAIT FOR YOU

I know that you're not ready yet—
    Your love I won't pursue;
But while you're making up your mind,
    My love will wait for you.

A love that's freely chosen
    Is a love that will endure.
A love that is prepared to wait
    Will end up more secure.

My love for you is something
    That I never will outgrow.
I'll wait until you're sure enough
    To answer yes or no.

And if you should decide that love
    Is not for us to share,
I hope that you will tell me so
    And your true thoughts declare.

But if you sense that love describes
    The feeling in your heart,
Then share with me your deepest thoughts
    So we're not long apart.

YOU'RE MORE THAN A FRIEND

I have a special feeling
    That I scarcely comprehend.
In my deepest thoughts I sense
    You're more than just a friend.

I wouldn't want to rush us now
    As friendship we explore;
But there's a growing warmth inside
    That I just can't ignore.

I enjoy our times together—
    We're so comfortable and free.
I think of you when I'm alone—
    I think of you and me.

I feel that we have much to share,
    Warm secrets to uncover.
There is a whole lot more to life
    That we can both discover.

I don't know where we're heading
    Or just where this road will end.
But you're truly someone special
    Who is more than just a friend.

TOGETHER

If life is full of challenge
    And gives us outstretched wings,
Let's soar to highest places
    And discover many things...
               together.

If life reveals its message
    To open eyes and ears,
Let's savor all the beauty
    And conquer any tears...
               together.

If life is meant for sharing
    And time forever runs,
Let's find our hidden moments
    And chase the setting sun...
               together.

If life is meant for loving
    And love is meant for two,
Let's never waste a moment
    Nor ever miss a cue...
               together.

If life is ever lonely
    And two are ever free,
Let us recall the moments
    When life placed you and me...
               together.

YOU'RE SO MUCH MORE

When I think of others
    I have met and known before,
Nothing in my thoughts compares with you —
    You're so much more.

I can't ignore the feelings
    That are rushing through my heart —
I feel we've been together
    Longer than we've been apart.

Our spirits seem to know each other;
    Thoughts exist in phase.
Life is pure sensation
    Softly shared a thousand ways.

A knowledge and a comfort
    Fills my feelings to the core.
I know that I am one with you,
    Because you're so much more.

SHARE WITH ME

Share with me your inner world;
    Reveal to me your thinking.
Tell me when your spirits soar,
    Or even when they're sinking.

Share with me your every mood.
    Permit me to explore
Your hopes and aspirations—
    Let me know you to the core.

Share with me your true concerns,
    Perplexities and fears.
Share your strengths and weaknesses...
    And don't conceal your tears.

Share with me your fantasies,
    Your loves and your obsessions.
Let me understand your wants
    And savor your impressions.

Let me know your inner warmth
    And share your inner flame.
Tell me all there is to know,
    And I will do the same.

SINCE WE MET

Since we met, I'm more alive —
   I see the days more clearly.
There's a glowing in my heart —
   I weigh the hours dearly.

Since we fully gave ourselves
   And touched in ways of caring,
We opened up the infinite,
   Unleashed the light of sharing.

You satisfy the hunger
   That inhabits hearts alone
And fill me with the passion
   That your tenderness has sown.

We fill a special space in time,
   A universe of two.
I share the world of now
   In heart and mind with only you.

NEW LOVE

Our love is young and has
   The fragile beauty of a rose;
But whether life will let
   Its form endure, time only knows.

If we allow these moments
   To inspire feelings new,
We'll gaze upon tomorrow
   As a time for me and you.

But if we fail to nourish
   The emotions love has built,
Then all its vital freshness
   Will too soon begin to wilt.

In this sweet moment I can't guess
   If love will choose to stay.
But I'm content to cherish
   Its rare form from day to day.

LEND ME LOVE

Lend me love
    And love me true
And lure me into
    Debt with you.

All the love that
    I can borrow
I'll repay before
    Tomorrow.

To the sum of
    Totals due
I'll add my highest
    Interest, too.

That way my payments
    Will accrue
As functions of
    My love for you.

Each time your heart
    Approves a loan,
I'll reimburse it
    From my own.

DANCE WITH ME

Dance with me and share my steps
    As we have done before.
Let us merge our forms in warmth
    And drift across the floor.

Flow with me in freedom,
    Let our routine movements vary.
Let's drink the music of the moment,
    Feel our motions marry.

Let's sweep our senses past
    The pounding threshold of our cares.
Let's glide in carefree comfort
    Upon light and buoyant airs.

Let's fuse in feelings physical,
    Escape in cloudless dreams.
Let's slip up to the heavens,
    Swept away on silver beams.

THROUGH OUR EYES

Through my eyes, look into me—
    See things no one has seen.
Gaze a while, see a smile,
    Let nothing come between.
Discover all and then some more;
    Find facets never found.
Let my eyes tell everything
    Without a single sound.

Through your eyes will I perceive
    The infinite in you—
The crystal maze that time surveys
    And life brings into view.
I'll gather in your brightest rays,
    Discover hidden talents;
I'll penetrate the mystery
    Of lives and hearts in balance.

I'll look at you and you at me—
    Our eyes will talk together.
Our meanings will traverse the air
    As softly as a feather.
We'll know the truth that words and deeds
    Don't have the time to tell;
And through our eyes shall I in you
    And you in me e'er dwell.

OUR UNIVERSE

Alone...
>I looked into the night
>and felt its cold.

Standing together...
>We saw the stars
>and were amazed.

Touching each other...
>We forgot darkness
>and discovered our own universe.

Sharing...
>We explored that universe
>and found it a warmer, better place.

Loving...
>We became aware
>of its infinite depth.

Growing together...
>We wanted our universe
>to endure.

Remaining together...
>We created a beautiful
>synthesis of our dreams.

THE KISS

Lips meet softly,
   Trading light pressures,
Sharing moist meanings
   In nerve-sweet moments.

Plump pat of love,
   Robbing breath,
Focusing pleasure,
   Warming the senses.

Tender point of contact,
   Stirring passion,
Arousing the heart
   In privileged surprise.

Caress my life fondly
   With private compulsions;
And tempt me to explore
   Your intimate secrets.

OUR SECRET LOVE

In inner space our lives embrace;
    In softness I discover
How you in sheltered moments
    Have become my friend, my lover.

In secret places love erases
    The innocence of friends.
In warming ways we touch in praise
    And closeness never ends.

In vision's eye our looks supply
    A feast of forms to know.
In sensual disclosure
    We have nothing left to show.

With intimate intentions,
    Through mutual desires,
For friendliest of reasons,
    My heart with yours conspires.

I NEED YOU

It seems you're always in my dreams—
    You fill my waking hours.
Your presence and your promise
    Warm me with their magic powers.

My heart's in disarray—My mind
    Is reeling with distraction.
My body feels for yours
    An irresistible attraction.

Whenever we're apart, that sense
    Of emptiness starts growing.
But when you're close to me
    My world is filled to overflowing.

My thoughts all lead to passion—
    My emotions fully heed you.
Each moment, every bit of me
    Keeps saying that I need you.

LISTEN TO MY HEART

Come close to me and let me show you
    Where my feelings start.
Come close to where affections flow
    And listen to my heart.

Remove the distance in between
    That makes us feel as two.
Let us press our hearts together,
    Vital links renew.

Magnify the force of love
    That bonds our life as one.
Let our chemistry together
    Be our inner sun.

Hear the pounding message
    Of two bodies taking part,
And let the word of love be spoken
    Softly to the heart.

TIME BEGAN WITH US

Was there a time
    When our fondest emotions
Ran free and untamed
    Like the most distant oceans?

Was there a moment
    In infinite space
When our hearts didn't mesh
    In a loving embrace?

Was there an instant
    In deepest recall
When our spirits and souls
    Weren't together at all?

Was there a past
    Before we had met
When loneliness summoned
    A sense of regret?

Despite all our yesterdays,
    I must confess—
The present is all
    That my heart can possess.

Our loving has conquered
    The past that's within.
When we found each other,
    Time chose to begin.

WE WERE MEANT TO BE

Certain chance occurrences
   Have caused our paths to meet.
Destiny has joined our hearts
   And made our lives complete.

Not all lives that cross
   Produce a union that is strong.
Fate can sometimes tempt
   And then remind us we were wrong.

Fortune has confirmed
   Our love is not a false disguise.
Love is something we in time
   Will truly maximize.

Something rare has happened —
   Life has given us a chance.
There is something natural
   And true in our romance.

Days are so delicious —
   Time is special; minds are free.
I believe our love is real
   And we were meant to be.

COME SHARE MY LIFE

I've wandered through the forest
    And heard its sounds alone.
I've seen a robin hopping
    And paused where moss has grown.

I've thrown a pebble seaward
    While walking on the sand.
I've sat and watched the waves break
    And gathered shells in hand.

I've seen the autumn colors
    And hiked through winter snow.
I've felt the summer rainfall
    And watched spring flowers grow.

I've savored life in moments past,
    But now I understand—
There's more to life if we can share it
    Walking hand in hand.

YOU ARE MY INSPIRATION

You are my inspiration,
My source of energy.
You stimulate my senses;
You set my spirits free.

You liberate my thinking;
You captivate my heart.
You redefine my vision;
You magnify my art.

You stir my independence;
You sentence me for life
To see your sweeter meanings—
You still the outer strife.

You bring me close to nature;
You share with me its truth.
You rush me into springtime;
You exercise my youth.

You make all time seem precious—
Life's essence you enhance.
You fill my days with wonder
And exquisite romance.

I'M FEELING CLOSE TO YOU

A message inside me,
    A feeling I know
Is stirring a warm
    And affectionate glow.

I'm feeling so close to you,
    Feeling so near,
That songs from my heart
    Are all that I hear.

Your spirit has drifted
    Right into my dreams.
I'm endlessly seeing
    Your image, it seems.

Our hearts are together;
    Our spirits are free;
We're drifting together
    So effortlessly.

No distance, no freedom
    Can draw us apart.
I'm closer to you where it counts—
    In the heart.

BEFORE I MET YOU

Before I met you I was just
    A lonely dream in flight,
A heart without an anchor,
    A season without light.

My hopes still craved an answer;
    My spirit sought to grow;
My life still needed someone
    To set my soul aglow.

But when the moment happened
    And we joined in heart and mind,
A life of new discovery
    Was tenderly defined.

We learned to walk the path of sharing—
    Talked and laughed and cared.
Our fondness for each other
    Was in truth and warmth declared.

And soon we knew that passion
    Was the gift that two receive
When they embrace the feeling
    That their love will never leave.

IF MY HEART COULD TALK

If my heart and mind could capture
    Feelings that I know
And speak them plainly,
    All the things I want to say would flow.

But I can never seem to find
    The phrases that I seek
To tell you softly everything
    My heart would like to speak.

Emotions resting in the heart
    Sustain and feed the soul.
Your presense in my life just seems
    To make my spirit whole.

But I cannot explain the thoughts
    That filter through my day.
Your meaning is much more to me
    Than words can ever say.

I LOVE YOUR MYSTERY

You're rather unpredictable;
    You're different, not the same—
A puzzle to decipher,
    A freest wind to tame.

I never hope to understand
    Your subtleties and shades.
Each time I chase your meaning,
    All my comprehension fades.

I never can predict exactly
    How you're going to act.
The only thing that's constant
    Is the way that you attract.

I'll never find the answers—
    All solutions you defy.
But since I love your mystery,
    It's fun for me to try.

A SECRET FEELING

A secret emotion,
    A most private feeling
Is stirring affections
    That I've been concealing.

My heart doesn't know
    Why these feelings have started.
My thoughts rush to sensuous
    Regions uncharted.

My dreams are not rational,
    Based on clear thinking.
My logic and reason
    Are rapidly shrinking.

I'm not in control
    Of my inner emotions.
I'm lost in a pack
    Of impossible notions.

My senses are drowning
    In passionate scenes.
I cannot quite fathom
    What all of this means.

You've entered my thinking —
    I'm no more the same.
I'm feeling distracted —
    You're clearly to blame!

LET ME INTO YOUR HEART

I want to bridge the lonely thought
    That you are you and I am I
By letting hopes of "us" and "we"
    Connect our worlds in warm reply.

I want to find a link with love
    So we can both consume its fire.
I want our hearts to be so close
    That we can satisfy desire.

I want the stillness found in peace,
    The joining of two minds.
I want the new discoveries
    Our life together finds.

I want my inner feelings
    To embrace the deeper you.
I want to stretch my vision,
    Bring to love a fuller view.

I want to fit into your dreams,
    Accept a broader part.
So let me into all you are,
    Especially your heart.

A CORNER OF MY HEART

A corner of my heart
    Will always be reserved for you.
A corner of my consciousness
    Lets all your light shine through.

A corner of my senses
    Cannot shed your touch and feel.
A corner of my world
    Is very fresh and very real.

A corner of my daily hopes and dreams
    Has you in mind.
A corner of each breathing moment
    Wants our breath combined.

A corner of my spirit
    Finds in you a place that's free.
Your corner of my life
    Is now a major part of me.

YOU ARE ON MY MIND

Something in my inner space
    Would like to bridge the miles.
Something in the way I miss you
    Seems the worst of trials.

Something in the feelings
    That are kindled in my heart
Stirs the warmth and then the cold
    Of knowing we're apart.

Something in my memory
    That teases me so much
Is trying to recapture
    The true essence of your touch.

Something in the fleeting thoughts
    That merge both joy and pain
Makes the passions of the heart
    Much harder to contain.

Something in my quiet moments
    Seems at once so dear
When thoughts of you can crystallize
    Into a joyful tear.

Something in the way the heart
    A ray of warmth can find
Reminds me of just how I feel
    When you are on my mind.

PROTECTIVE SPIRITS

I kept guard over you
    In my thoughts,
Feeling that you were safer
    When you were close to my day.

It wasn't a conscious act
    Of remembering that kept you there,
Just the simple fact that
    When we're not together,
        We're not truly apart.

Your tender touch upon my time
    Wings me through my day,
Gliding me through routine moments
    With soft millisecond glimpses
        Into the shelter of your countenance.

Strange that the protective spirit
    I maintain for you
Seems to reflect your presence
    Back into my day
        And offer me comfort and security.

I hope your day benefits as mine,
    Being a little less lonely,
Feeling a little safer, a little more secure,
    By knowing that you're my heart's concern...
        And also my heart's solace.

THOUGHTS OF YOU AND ME

Today I thought
    Of you and me
In morning mists
    Of reverie.

I carried you
    Through later hour
In passing sun
    And warming shower.

I brought you
    To observe my day
And hoped that
    In my thoughts you'd stay.

With people
    And in solitude,
I found you sharing
    Every mood.

And after all
    Was done and said,
Your heart in tow
    Put mine to bed.

WHERE IN THE HEART?

Where in the heart do I find you?
　　Where in the mind do you rest?
Where in the focus of springtime
　　Do we join in one beautiful quest?

Where in the steep path of living
　　Do our patterns of life overlap?
Where in the course of our caring
　　Do we journey without any map?

Where in the realm of our senses
　　Do we merge into one vital form?
Where in the moments of hardship
　　Do we challenge together the storm?

Where in a passionate worldly embrace
　　Does our consciousness soar high above?
In the ever mysterious bondage,
　　That freedom of spirit called love.

I'M LOSING SLEEP OVER YOU

Sometimes when I go to bed
    And try in every way
To get a decent night of rest,
    Forget a tiring day,

I discover I'm not drifting
    Into slumber deep—
I'm just staring at the ceiling
    Wishing I could sleep.

You are very often why
    I miss my bedtime cues.
Thoughts of you account for almost
    All the sleep I lose.

I am so aware of you
    That when I sleep it seems
You occupy and heighten
    My most satisfying dreams.

But when it seems I'm lacking
    Just the right amount of you,
Sleeping is the exercise
    My mind won't let me do.

I WILL MISS YOU

You are the bright ingredient
　　In every passing day
That life and change and circumstance
　　Now softly steal away.

You're moving to the future,
　　Hitching to a distant star.
The goals that you are following
　　Are taking you afar.

My heart will travel with you,
　　And my hopes will bless your course.
My world of joy reluctantly
　　Bids farewell to its source.

That's not to say that thoughts of you
　　Won't lighten every day.
But now I look with longing
　　For that extra special ray.

Your presence is a luxury
　　My memory enshrines.
The sun is not as vivid
　　When your image elsewhere shines.

But for each empty feeling
　　That my lonely heart must learn
There is the corresponding joy
　　That comes when you return.

YOU'RE JUST A THOUGHT AWAY

Distance takes us far apart
    And darkens my today.
I have to keep remembering—
    You're just a thought away.

When the world is too confusing,
    Times are hard to bear,
I pull your precious meaning,
    Your bright spirit, from the air.

If I sometimes drift into
    A lonely state of mind,
I gather up the memories
    Of days we left behind.

And though you're not beside me,
    I can tap into my heart
And draw upon the warmth and love
    That lives when we're apart.

And with these fond reflections
    On the times when you were near,
I sense a little bit of what
    It's like to have you here.

WHEN WE ARE APART

In matters of the heart
    I have a weakness that is clear—
I can't imagine loneliness
    As long as you are near.

But when I can't be with you
    And I'm feeling all alone,
The sense of isolation
    Is the greatest I have known.

While we are close together,
    I am blissfully aware
That I am truly happy
    Merely knowing you are there.

But when we are apart,
    The very opposite is true—
I am totally distracted
    Merely knowing there is you.

I MISS YOU

A little bit of you
    And a little bit of me
Have switched respective places
    In a mystifying " we."

When miles come between us
    And our lives are drawn apart,
Our thoughts remain together
    Tugging softly at the heart.

This loneliness without you
    Tells of special moments shared
And says across the miles
    Just how much we've always cared.

The emptiness that comes
    With just the memory of your touch
Stirs a feeling from within that says,
    " I miss you very much."

YOU FILL MY THOUGHTS

In tender ways
  I often find
You fill my thoughts—
  You're on my mind.

In cherished moments
  I can sense
You give my thoughts
  Their eloquence.

In fond reflections
  Through the day
I think of you
  In every way.

In fleeting glimpses
  Of the past
The thoughts of you
  Are those that last.

In times apart
  I've always known
Through thoughts of you
  I'm not alone.

I'M THINKING OF YOU

My mind is moving silently,
  Fond memories selecting.
I linger long with thoughts of you,
  Remembering, reflecting.

In moments when the mind is free
  It makes impromptu choices;
And as it drifts from thought to thought
  It summons certain voices.

When time permits my thoughts to drift
  Through tides of fond recall,
I recreate the times we've shared,
  Those moments large and small.

And when I'm roused from reverie,
  An inner feeling yearns
For many more such moments
  When the thought of you returns.

WITH YOU, I'M ME

With you I feel that I can be
    Spontaneous and free.
I open up my heart to you
    In simple honesty.

I share with you my inner thoughts,
    Abandon all disguises.
I bare my deepest feelings,
    Shunning pretense or surprises.

I stand before you as I am,
    My strengths and flaws revealed.
No attitudes are hidden;
    No motives are concealed.

With you I'm free to be myself,
    Voice my identity.
I draw from you an inner calm
    That says—with you, I'm me.

WE NEED EACH OTHER

There's a simple mathematics,
    So absolute and true,
That says that one and one will always
    End up being two.

But there's another set of laws
    With love and life its source
That says two lives together
    Can unleash a vital force.

I know that we have found this force—
    Our spirits truly blend.
We've tapped an inner freedom—
    On each other we depend.

We've found that special meaning—
    We can cherish every hour.
We've discovered our own formula,
    Revealed an inner power—

That chemistry of sharing,
    That higher math of hearts
Whose sum of total being
    Is much greater than its parts.

SOMETHING HAPPENED IN MY HEART

Something happened in my heart
    A breath or two ago.
Its rhythm skipped and raced a bit
    And caused an inner glow.

I lost a breath as I drew in
    A fleeting thought of you.
I held the thought inside me—
    Then I let it filter through.

The warmth that it awakened,
    The feelings that it stirred
Gently notified me
    Something special had occurred.

For as I drew into my heart
    Your image passing through,
I knew that I had lost a breath
    And skipped a beat for you.

HAPPY BIRTHDAY, SWEETHEART

This day was meant for you, my love—
    You're all that I am thinking of.
There's nothing I would rather do
    Than spend this special time with you.

Your birthday will fond memories fill;
    But in our feelings time stands still.
Our life together turns a page;
    But in our hearts love has no age.

Togetherness is our true vow—
    We're living in a sacred now.
We value all the things we share—
    Our perfect space is everywhere.

This birthday wish tells how I feel—
    My love for you is very real.
It seems the proper time to say—
    I love you, dear, in every way.

YOU ARE MY POETRY

An image growing stronger,
    A metaphor increasing,
My source of inspiration,
    You are my love unceasing.

A mood I want to capture,
    A feeling to explore,
A message from inside me,
    A thought I can't ignore.

A need to know you further,
    To let my heart expound,
A hunger to describe the inner
    Beauty I have found.

You are my heart's creation;
    You set my verses free;
You are the words I'm looking for;
    You are my poetry.

HONEYSUCKLE

Honeysuckle satisfaction,
    Honeysuckle savor.
Honeysuckle sense of sweetness,
    Filling me with flavor.

Honeysuckle perfume,
    Unannounced in your seduction,
Floating in so freely,
    Never needing introduction.

Never could I love another
    As I now love you.
No nectar to my lips
    Could match your purity so true.

And once I've sipped your faint aroma
    To intoxication,
No flower less than yours
    Will stir my fond anticipation.

DEWDROP

Life is like a flower;
    Hope is like a tear;
Love is like a dewdrop
    Awaiting to appear.

Morning is the sunlight,
    The mist a passing haze,
The dew a fragile meeting,
    A meshing with the days.

Night defines the daylight;
    It changes dew to tear;
It closes up the flower;
    It opens hope to fear.

But while the flower's open
    And dew adorns its petals,
Let's celebrate the flower
    Until the teardrop settles.

SPRING VISIT

You came to me
  On perfumed day
When spring awoke
  In early May.

You came to me
  In budding birth,
In clusters closely
  Hugging earth.

You came to me
  In whispered breeze,
In luscious wind
  And waving trees.

You came to me
  In trilling song,
In sounds to which
  The days belong.

You came to me
  In hopeful rain
And warmed the heart
  And eased the pain.

YOU TURN ME ON

I'm a captive,
    I'm a pawn
To moments when
    You turn me on.

You stir my senses,
    Fill my mind,
Unleash my passions,
    Make me blind.

You're the strongest
    Of all potions.
You're the key
    To my emotions.

You will it, want it,
    Seek it, take it,
Show it, flaunt it,
    Can't forsake it.

You're an adult;
    You're a child;
You're the one
    Who makes me wild!

I'M CRAZY OVER YOU

Sometimes I'm crazy, distracted, confounded
    And climbing the walls over you.
No matter the season, the day or the reason,
    These feelings I just can't subdue.

I'm babbling, billowing, bubbling over—
    I'm feeling berserk and unstable.
I can't get a grip on myself or my feelings—
    When I try to calm down, I'm unable.

I'm out of this world with excitement.
    I'm feeling mixed up through and through.
I'm high in the sky and I'm crazy—
    I'm wildly insane about you.

I AM YOURS

The intimate surrender
    My captive heart explores
Permits me to confess
    My deepest feeling—"I am yours."

The loving balance that allows
    Two spirits to combine
Tells my heart to grasp
    The gentle concept, "You are mine."

The limits of our love,
    The widest bounds of our affection,
Attach the fullest meaning to
    Our dreams and our direction.

And when our deep commitment
    Finds a challenge to withstand,
The definition of our love
    Is ready to expand.

"I am yours" is my true pledge,
    Not just a groundless phrase.
My heart is poised with yours
    To plot our love a thousand ways.

THE FORCE OF TWO

My love for you is part of me —
    It leads me through each day.
It blends with every conscious thought
    And softly shows the way.

It frees me from concern
    And gives my dreams a tender base.
Whenever you are near,
    The world is easier to face.

My love for you completes
    The highest circle of my heart
And tells me that your role
    Has turned into a leading part.

You give my deeper feelings
    And my warmth a place to grow.
You lift my spirits to the sky,
    Release an inner glow.

Your love allows my passions
    To explore the force of two
And redefines in countless precious ways
    My love for you.

A DAY WITHOUT YOU

It's hard to imagine
      A sky without blue,
A spring without flowers,
      A day without you.

You're so much a part
      Of my landscape of living
That I take for granted
      The treasures you're giving.

But if I attempt
      To absorb all your light
And see how your colors
      Illumine the night,

I realize that all
      That my heart reads as true
Is lost if the day
      Is a day without you.

FOREVER AND ALWAYS

Forever and always
  Our love will endure.
Our hopes will grow stronger,
  Our thoughts more secure.

Forever and always.
  Time will recall
The heat of our passion,
  The start of it all.

Forever and always,
  Through darkness and light,
The days will be rich
  With the promise of night.

Forever and always
  Our spirits will blend;
Our hearts will join forces,
  Soft messages send.

Forever and always
  Our dreams will continue;
And all that I'm looking for
  I'll find within you.

YOU'RE MY FANTASY

You are my favored fantasy,
  My island of discovery.
You elevate my spirits—
  You're my reason for recovery.

You stir my fond imaginings,
  Give reverie its fuel.
You brighten every moment—
  You're my ever precious jewel.

You stimulate my senses;
  You're the center of my thinking.
You give me hope and optimism,
  Keep my faith from shrinking.

You tutor me in passion,
  Give substance to my dreams.
You fill up my emotions,
  Let me love you to extremes.

You and I are lovers
  In that land within the heart.
Let's hope it's ours forever;
  Let's hope we'll never part.

LOVE IS A RAINBOW

Love is a rainbow
    Where true colors blend.
You are the treasure
    I find at the end.

Love is our spectrum
    Of thoughts and emotions,
Our feelings of warmth
    And affectionate notions.

Love's our invisible
    Visible force—
Our ultimate, infinite,
    Exquisite source.

Love is our fantasy
    Glimmering bright,
Life's beautiful image
    Reflecting the light.

Love is our dream
    That wants to come true—
I'm glad to be sharing
    This rainbow with you.

MY LOVE FOR YOU

My love for you
    Is like the sky,
With dreams that soar
    And hopes that fly.

It's like a
    Never ending ocean,
An everlasting,
    Deep emotion.

It has the tenderness
    Of spring,
The charm that warmth
    And laughter bring.

It has the simple
    Strength of stone.
It shields us from
    A life alone.

It's ever growing,
    Ever new.
It's always there,
    My love for you.

FOREVER US

"Alone" is a word
  That appeals to me never.
"Us" is our concept,
  Our feeling forever.

Time has a strange
  And magnificent motion.
Love is the meaning —
  The tide in this ocean.

Each individual
  Struggles to find
A partner in body,
  A match for the mind.

My searching is over —
  Love's tide has pulled in.
Now is the moment
  For time to begin.

Time is our ally —
  Life's so appealing.
We're locked through the ages
  Forever in feeling.

Hope is our candle;
  Love is our guide.
Our hearts say "forever us"
  Deep down inside.

THANKS FOR LOVING ME

My life was once a game of chance,
    A solitary quest,
A lonely search for someone
    Who could fill my world the best.

But then my heart discovered
    Something pure and something free:
The love I felt for you
    And all that you expressed for me.

You were the substance of my dreams
    So softly coming true.
You saw as much within my soul
    As I perceived in you.

It's sometimes hard to love
    Unless another feels the same.
You let the sparks of true affection
    Mirror back a flame.

When love fills one, it may remain
    A possibility.
When love fills two, dreams can come true —
    So, thanks for loving me.

WE HAVE EACH OTHER

We may at times feel lacking in
   The luxuries of living,
But luxuries cannot compare
   With all that life is giving.

We have our lives together;
   We have our shared affection;
We have the hopes and aspirations
   Of a shared direction.

We have the riches of the heart,
   Of family and friends.
We have respect for one another
   That our loving lends.

We have the comfort of just knowing
   That someone is near.
We have the reassurance
   Of a sympathetic ear.

We have the bounties of each day,
   Events both large and small.
Through all the moments that we share,
   We really have it all.

I LOVE YOU MORE EACH DAY

I saw you again today
    For the first time.
Love, you see, has a way of letting us
    Rediscover yesterday's surprises.

Tomorrow, I'll again be alert to you—
    Your words, your appearance,
    Your movement, your touch—
For I'm certain there's something
    I missed today.

Each day I want to discover
    All there is to discover;
But each succeeding day
    My discovery begins anew.

FOR MY LOVE

I searched my world for you...
Uncertain of your existence,
I hoped, but sometimes doubted, that I would find you.
I now feel the pressure lifted.
I look and still see those around me;
But my looking and seeing are an affirmation
Of my discovery of you.
As time passes, the gift of chance that you represent
Becomes even more evident and striking.
The improbability of *us*
As a function of life's chance encounters
Frightens me;
Because if you had not been there when I was,
Or I had not been there when you were,
We wouldn't have found
That miracle of warmth and completeness we now feel.
Were this gift not ours,
Were you not mine,
I would still be searching for you
As a boat in fog seeks its mooring,
As a swimmer his landfall,
As an airborne seed its permanent base of growth.

YOU AND I

You and I,
    A special phrase,
That warms the night
    And lights the days.

You and I,
    A concept true,
That speaks of love
    And visions new.

You and I,
    A precious time,
A gentle thought,
    A tender rhyme.

You and I,
    Two hearts that care,
Two minds that mesh,
    Two lives that share.

Love and hope
    And sun and sky
Now whisper dreams
    Of you and I.

I LOVE YOU

I'm thinking, dreaming,
    Conscious of you,
Feeling, knowing
    That I love you.

I'm sensing, seeing
    How you haunt me,
Wishing, hoping
    That you want me.

I'm noting, minding
    How I heed you,
Contemplating
    That I need you.

I'm witnessing
    Through waves and oceans
How you govern
    My emotions.

No thought I have
    Exists above you.
In my heart I know
    I love you.

I'M SECURE IN YOU

There are things the heart won't question,
  Sensations so secure,
That they exist in mind and flesh,
  In primal regions pure.

They have the strength of granite,
  The softness of a touch,
The full persuasion of a flower,
  The warmth that means so much.

I cannot take for granted
  That such treasures are my due.
Instead I'm awed and thankful
  That I feel secure in you.

Such chemistry does not result
  From feeble fascination.
It's active; it's dynamic;
  It needs loving affirmation.

The confidence I feel in you
  Is my profoundest praise.
My love for you will thrive in me
  And brighten all my days.

LOVE IS ALWAYS THERE

The life we lead,
    The hopes we share
Remind us love
    Is always there.

When roads we walk
    Appear uphill,
We demonstrate
    A patient will.

When life's dilemmas
    Pass us by,
We celebrate
    A cloudless sky.

The dullest trip
    Would always be
On flattest land
    Our quiet sea.

But how enchanting
    Is the quest
That sometimes puts us
    To the test.

And how exciting
    Is the find
When lives are fondly
    Intertwined.

YOU ARE MY STAR

You are my star
    Shining ever so bright.
You walk with the sun;
    You challenge the night.

You guide me through darkness,
    Chase shadows by day.
You force all the problems
    Of living away.

You warm by your presence;
    You lift up my moods.
You raise me in spirit
    To high altitudes.

You light up my thinking;
    You charm every hour.
You summon within me
    A much higher power.

You color my future,
    Cast rainbows afar.
You're my stellar body—
    Yes, you are my star.

YOU'RE PERFECT IN MY EYES

Like clouds across the sunset,
    A moon in starry skies,
A rainfall in the springtime—
    You're perfect in my eyes.

All beauty has its shades and tones,
    Each gem a form that's raw.
Each diamond has a subtle way
    Of mirroring its flaw.

I see you as the misty mask
    Enshrouding early day.
I see you as the wildflower
    Nuzzling grass away.

I see you as a naked form
    With memory's lonely scars.
I see you as a feeling
    That no inner knowledge mars.

I see you as temptation
    Casting off your scant disguise.
I see you as a natural—
    You're perfect in my eyes.

LOVE IS...

Love is finding that with you
    Each simple thing is something new,
Each winter hour is full of spring,
    Each moment is worth cherishing.

It's feeling in your presence free
    And knowing that with you I'm me.
It's finding comfort at your side
    And seeking moments to confide.

It's sensing darkness when you're gone
    Yet knowing night must yield to dawn.
It's feeling snug when we're together
    And finding calm in any weather.

It's feeling youth at every age.
    It's being rich despite your wage.
It's feeling happy, seldom blue;
    But, darling, most of all it's you!

ALL I WANT IS YOU

I'll tell it rather simply;
    I'll say it plain and true—
A single thing is all I want;
    And all I want is you.

There are no other riches,
    No treasures or possessions
That ever could compare with you,
    My fondest of obsessions.

You are the very air I breathe,
    The ration that sustains me.
You're all my thoughts tied up as one,
    The laugh that entertains me.

You're all that life need ever give,
    The maximum that's due.
If I could ask for anything,
    I'd only ask for you.

MARRIAGE OF TWO HEARTS

In every heart there is a spark
    That wants to be a flame.
In every life there is a part
    That only love can tame.

In every day there is a moment
    Eager to be shared.
In every mind a tender thought
    Just waits to be declared.

In every forest there's a trail
    Which two can happier roam.
In every place there is a spot
    Which two can call a home.

In every joy a higher gladness
    Reigns if there are two.
In every love there is the hope
    That dreams will all come true.

In every marriage of two hearts
    Two lives exist as one.
In every journey that two share
    Life's really just begun.

MY WIFE, MY LOVE

My wife, my love, my dearest friend,
  You've given me your heart to tend.
I've given you my life to share;
  My heart is in your tender care.

My wife, my hope, my fondest dream,
  We form a true devoted team.
In all the moments life may bring,
  You are my star, my everything.

My wife, my source of lasting truth,
  You stir in me eternal youth;
You give my heart a sense of pride;
  You fuel my warmest thoughts inside.

My wife, my daily inspiration,
  You're the love in my equation.
You're my source of deep affection.
  You're my compass and direction.

THE MESSAGE OF OUR MARRIAGE

The message of our marriage
    Started softly with a kiss.
The meaning of the moment
    Spoke a truth we couldn't miss.

The fact about the future
    Was that you and I were one.
The loneliness and isolation
    Of the past were done.

The ritual of joining
    Hearts together left us shining.
We traded vows of hope and trust,
    Through love our souls combining.

Our rings embraced commitment,
    Circled lives, let spirits mend.
Upon our fingers they inscribed
    A future without end.

The promise of together
    Left a treasure for tomorrow.
The warmth of you and me became
    A strength from which to borrow.

ANNIVERSARY OF OUR LOVE

Let's recall that moment
　　When our love had just begun,
That special place in time
　　When all our hopes were joined as one.

Let us now reflect upon
　　The precious past we feel,
The tender anniversary
　　Our hearts embrace as real.

Let's remember all that happened
　　In our lives that day
To send a deeper message
　　Of devotion that would stay.

Let's affirm that all we know
　　Of love and true affection
Started flowing when our dreams
　　Assumed the same direction.

And now as I look back
　　At how our early passions grew,
I celebrate and cherish
　　My discovery of you.

THE PERFECT TWO

If I define the number *two*,
    There's just one meaning, me and you.
If I explain the pronoun *we*,
    I'm struck with thoughts of you and me.
If I explore the small word *us*,
    I see it lasting ever thus.
If I reflect on life *together*,
    I see no hint of stormy weather.

If there's a chance you share my view
    And see in us the perfect *two*
And feel quite free
    In using *we*
And give a plus
    To dreams of *us*,
Then possibly heart's fragile tether
    Will keep the two of us *together*.

OUR LOVE

Our love is something we have built
    From passions, hopes and dreams.
It's safe from any passing moods,
    Secure from all extremes.

It's something real and special,
    Something solid, something pure.
It's something we can always count on,
    Ringing sound and sure.

It's something grounded in the heart,
    Emitting confidence.
It lives in our emotions;
    It is something we can sense.

Our love remains a binding force,
    Resistant to all strife.
Amidst the outer pressures,
    It's our anchor throughout life.

THANKS FOR ALWAYS BEING THERE

The world is moving faster now —
    We're on a changing course.
But you have helped me deal with life —
    You've been a stable force.

When I have had to follow
    New directions, you were there.
When the world was hard on me,
    You always seemed to care.

When nothing held together,
    Made the slightest bit of sense,
You have always helped restore
    My inner confidence.

Everyone needs someone
    Who's reliable and true.
Through the moments I've endured,
    I'm grateful there was you.

OUR RELATIONSHIP IS SPECIAL

Our relationship is special;
　　Our friendship is the best.
Our love is ever growing;
　　Our life's a wondrous quest.

We share all things together;
　　We never feel alone.
We look at all we've been through;
　　We look at how we've grown.

We grasp the tender moments,
　　The times we spend as one.
We savor our accomplishments,
　　The projects we've begun.

We think of how much better
　　Life flows as you and me.
We can't escape the loving thought
　　That we were meant to be.

I BELIEVE IN US

I believe in thoughts we share,
    In feelings we discuss.
I believe in magic moments—
    I believe in us.

I believe in sunny days,
    The warming touch of rain.
I believe in special times
    That form an endless chain.

I believe in quiet nights,
    In vivid starlit skies.
I believe in tender sights
    That stir romantic eyes.

I believe in positives,
    In truths that form a plus.
I believe in love and sharing—
    I believe in us.

THE ONE I LOVE

The one I love is all I need
    To set my heart ablaze.
The one I love's the center of
    My life in many ways.

The one I love is part of me,
    Companion to my dreams,
And is the main ingredient
    In all my thoughts, it seems.

The one I love supports me through
    The challenges I face
And knows the healing power
    Of a warm and fond embrace.

The one I love responds to me,
    My spirits can renew.
The one I love is full of passion;
    The one I love is you!

A TIME FOR US

In a little space amidst the hurry
    Where the world is free of fuss,
Let's share a moment all our own—
    A special time for us.

Let's shape a quiet interlude,
    Explore our inner being.
Let's see ourselves as only we
    Are capable of seeing.

Let's rediscover hidden moments,
    Times of you and me.
Let's recreate the moods we've known,
    So sensuous and free.

Let's bring our lives together,
    Find the warmth that means so much.
Let's draw our beating hearts so close
    That they can almost touch.

And after hearts have spoken
    And this special time has fled,
A silent closeness, calm and sure,
    Will fill our hearts instead.

I WANT YOU

In a peaceful, perfect moment,
    In a mood of gentle giving,
Let's flow into each other,
    Turn each other on to living.

In a free and open manner,
    In a ritual of senses,
Let's cast off inhibition
    And abandon our defenses.

In a scene of sensuality,
    In the confidence of sharing,
Let's tease and touch and tantalize
    And be a little daring.

In the fullest self-expression,
    In the peace of perfect pleasure,
Let's fuse our hearts together
    And explore love's tender treasure.

I NEED A HUG

At the end of a lengthy
   And tiring day
When I've faced the world
   In my private way,
            I need a hug!

When I'm hungry and cranky
   And feeling up tight
And a day has just passed
   When too little went right,
            I need a hug!

When my body is craving
   The warmth of another
And my poor aching muscles
   Compete with each other,
            I need a hug!

When I'm insecure
   And a little bit nutty
And my mind is exhausted,
   My body like putty,
            I need a hug!

When I am affectionate,
   Loving and caring
And want to enjoy
   A real moment of sharing,
            I need a hug!

YOU WARM UP MY TOES

You warm my feet,
    Revive my toes;
You cure my chilly
    Bedtime woes.

You make the dark
    Fill up with light.
You make a comfy
    Place of night.

You touch me softly,
    Nuzzle, press
And chase away
    My loneliness.

I feel your form
    As part of mine.
As we reach out,
    Our hearts combine.

Your slumber stirs
    A loving laugh
When you sprawl out
    And hog my half.

And I drink in
    Our warmth as lovers,
Though you at times
    Grab all my covers.

LOVE IS A WORD

Love is a word
    With a sensible sound,
Yet its use makes a sensible
    Head go around.

For it seems that this word
    Can have multiple uses
Which sometimes can lead
    To more subtle abuses.

This says to a sensitive,
    Critical heart
That the language of love
    Is a language apart.

The use of the word
    Affords no real assurance
That the feeling behind it
    Has chance of endurance.

So love can't depend
    On an audible sound,
For the silence of love
    Is a silence profound;

And the actions that help
    In defining this word
Go beyond any message
    So easily heard.

I'M SENSITIVE TO YOU

I'm influenced in many ways
    By things you say and do.
I guess, to put it simply,
    I am sensitive to you.

This means that deep inside my heart
    I've made a conscious choice
To weigh your words with care
    And know each nuance of your voice.

This is the highest compliment,
    The truest sign of love.
It shows that as I live my life
    You're what I'm thinking of.

In giving you complete and total
    Access to my heart,
I focus in on certain feelings
    You alone impart.

This means your words will always have
    A powerful effect.
I may react to things you say
    In ways you don't expect.

I hope that you will understand
    We have so much to share.
If ever I react to you,
    It's just because I care.

LOVE WILL FIND A WAY

Two people can feel very close,
    Their honest love proclaim,
Yet also know that they're free spirits,
    Not at all the same.

Such people need a little room
    To let their spirits speak.
They can't suppress the differences
    That make them so unique.

Freedom exercised with taste
    Can help two people grow.
It helps them understand themselves,
    Lets deeper talents show.

Though two may give each other space,
    No loss of love's to blame,
For they have merely recognized
    They're different, not the same.

A positive conclusion
    Is much easier to assume
When two have found enough respect
    To give each other room.

LOVE MAKES IT WORK

We needn't pretend that it's perfect,
　　Nor dwell on the fact that it's not.
We needn't expect a relationship
　　Devoid of all blemish or spot.

It's normal to be a bit human:
　　Some problems are part of the game.
Things would be hopelessly boring
　　If, flawlessly, we were the same.

But still it's important to notice,
　　No matter how human we are,
That love is the measure of progress:
　　It leads us and guides us afar.

We don't have to worship perfection,
　　Nor give up all struggle for change;
But love can be perfect when we're not—
　　It's a gift we can proudly exchange.

PLEASE SAVE SOME TIME FOR ME

The time we share has grown too scarce;
    Our special moments flee.
Though life has its required tasks,
    Please save some time for me.

There are so many routine things
    To occupy our days
It's often hard to meet within
    The center of our maze.

We give a lot of extra effort
    To the things we do
And often spend our energies
    Alone and not as two.

And when our first free moment
    Then becomes a date to keep,
Our need to share competes with our
    More basic need for sleep.

My batteries need charging;
    I'm short of energy.
I want to share my life with you—
    Please save some time for me.

I NEED A LITTLE YOU

I need a little you
  To make the day a little brighter.
I need a little you
  To make my duties seem much lighter.

I need a little you
  To help me see life's faults and face them.
I need a little you
  To take my problems and erase them.

I need a little you
  To want to share my company.
I need a little you
  To need a little bit of me.

I need a little you
  To draw so close that I can squeeze you.
I need a little you,
  Because I want the chance to please you.

I need a little you
  So I have someone to adore.
I need a little you,
  But I could really use much more.

YOU ARE JUST A PART OF ME

In after hours' quiet darkness,
    Letting thoughts unwind,
I fuse with you in form
    And drink your warmth into my mind.

I draw your spirit closer,
    Taking in your gentle feeling.
I let our pressures softly blend
    And fill our hearts with healing.

We're but a single shape,
    A moving still life of positions.
We fill opposing curves
    And whisper silent recognitions.

We're unified in touch
    And feel a wondrous sense of "we."
I pull you in so close
    That you are just a part of me.

BREATH OF NIGHT

You fell asleep before me —
    Now you drift in upward breezes.
You're like a seed borne into flight
    That each new current teases.

Your peace in free fall slumber
    Lifts you up into the sky.
Your breath propels you further
    As you slip into a sigh.

I feel your warming presence
    As I watch your spirit soar.
I sense the upper reaches
    You so earnestly explore.

I see the gentle air on which
    You float without a frown
And hope the winds of freedom
    Will softly set you down.

A QUIET KISS GOOD NIGHT

Sometimes love is simple
    In its needs,
Existing with no call for
    Special deeds.

The nighttime stillness
    Of two nesting birds
Is shared in us when we
    Relinquish words.

We lie in quiet moments
    Side by side
Allowing but our presence
    To provide.

And then to seal
    The warmth upon the night,
Our lips search out
    A quiet kiss good night.

IF YOU HAD SAID GOOD NIGHT

You left me to myself
    And to the thoughts that I was facing.
Your breath and body slowed to sleep —
    My heart and mind were racing.

I couldn't stand to be alone
    Without a moment's parting.
Your day was winding down
    And yet my night was sadly starting.

I needed someone's softness
    To adjourn my day to dreaming.
You slipped away so quietly
    Your silence left me steaming.

I wish that you had sensed
    My simple need for interaction
And didn't leave me all alone
    To fight the night's distraction.

My lonely state of mind,
    Intent on darkness, craved your light.
It would have been much easier
    If you had said good night.

I WANT YOUR LOVE

I want to feel your love for me,
    To sense your warm desire.
I want to know that deep within you
    Embers turn to fire.

I want to see your senses
    Lifted up on passion's wave.
I want to feel your hunger
    For the very things I crave.

I want my heart and mind
    To stir your mind and heart together
And let our tender feelings
    Float the currents like a feather.

I want to touch your body,
    Plot each feature of your form,
Caress the softer details,
    Let emotions gently storm.

I want to merge our movement
    Into one magnetic motion.
I want the fluid force of love
    To build into an ocean.

THAT ENERGY CALLED LOVE

That physical focus,
  That river of heart,
That moment of mutual
  Magical art.

The tactile encounter,
  The total surrender,
The feeling of fusion,
  The sipping of splendor.

The tasting and testing,
  The trying and trading,
The helping, assisting,
  Exploring and aiding.

The limitless loving,
  The endless profusion,
The sensuous searching,
  Defying conclusion.

The energy flooding,
  The warmth overflowing,
The passion expanding,
  The dialog growing.

That moment, that minute—
  Obsessive, unending—
When the energy found in two lovers
  Is blending.

FAMILIAR GLANCES

Familiar glances lengthened to a stare
    As I absorbed your figure standing there.
The many times you'd stood before my eyes
    Did not reduce the moment's soft surprise.

I felt a little shy to linger so
    But somehow didn't want the time to go.
I knew you wouldn't mind the eyes' caress,
    The touch of vision only I possess.

For me you are no less a work of art,
    Though countless times your view
        Has crossed my heart.
These private moments, purely off the cuff,
    Refresh the soul but never are enough.

With quiet, fleeting thoughts too quick to share,
    My inner feelings penetrate the air;
But sometimes the attraction of your form
    Compels me to reach out and share your warm.

VISUAL POETRY

Your flowing ripe lines of familiar flesh
    Punctuate my vision.
My seasoned eyes return again
    To caress their plenty.

Their fullness frees desire.
    Their roundness perfectly attracts
And tempts my lips
    With their soft gentle sweep.

I train my eyes unselfconsciously
    In loving tribute
To the memories of touch
    So warmly teasing.

My glance drinks in this vintage feeling.
    My arms complete the tactile circuit,
Drawing your near form to my lips,
    To my own press of flesh.

What was imagined now turns real.
    What vision incited loses its clamor.
What memory impressed impresses again.
    What was poetry in motion newly inspires
        And transforms this audience of one.

STAY CLOSE TO ME

When morning sun is beaming
   On our silhouetted love
And as I stir I know that
   You are all I'm thinking of,
              Stay close to me.

When birds commence their songs of love
   And sound their soft alarm
And, lacking inhibition,
   We are tangled arm in arm,
              Stay close to me.

When comfort streams between two bodies
   Welded side to side
And when there are no secrets
   For familiar forms to hide,
              Stay close to me.

When touching is a tactile treasure
   We can both explore
And we can sense each other's
   Inner appetite for more,
              Stay close to me.

When love's a true collaboration,
   Perfect with its flaws,
A joy that needs elaboration,
   Thriving "just because,"
              Stay close to me.

When every mood we share
   Is but an exercise in love
And two unique identities
   Can fit just like a glove,
              Stay close to me.

When we can still experiment,
   Discover something new,
And all the mystery of love
   Is there when I'm with you,
                  Stay close to me.

When we can watch the setting sun
   With optimistic eyes
And learn to love the night
   Before the sun begins to rise,
                  Stay close to me.

SILENCE SHARED

Listening to silence,
   We sat in the distilled quiet
      Of our thoughts.
We didn't mind the empty moments
   And didn't try to fill them.

Our free associations dashed
   In unguarded randomness,
Unweighted by guilt,
   Unmoved by lost conversation.

This freedom not to talk,
   This comfort in each other,
Signed with sealed lips
   A statement about love
That justified any idle words
   We may have missed.

WHEN TIME STANDS STILL

The crystalline perfection
    Of a moment locked in time
Distills its true reflection
    Into memory sublime.

A day when progress halted
    And time, it seemed, stood still,
We sipped of pure simplicity
    And couldn't get our fill.

We focused on the plainer truths;
    We saw with clearer eyes;
We shunned the clutter in our lives
    And thus became more wise.

Life has certain jewels
    That are timeless and are rare.
They captivate us humbly
    In a breath of pure spring air.

A SPACE IN TIME

A crack in true eternal time
    Gives window to existence.
Mortal eyes so poignantly
    Record this precious distance.

Our brief moment lets us love
    This fragile gift of chance,
Filling eyes abundantly
    With life's resplendent glance.

Light my vision with awareness
    Of each fleeting second.
Let my senses shower
    In the warmth of hearts that beckoned.

Let us fill this crack in time
    And occupy our space
In such a way that time will say—
    Now, endlessly embrace.

THE FLOWER

An understated majesty
    In every flower grows.
In humankind the blossoming
    Of souls through kindness shows.

Examples sown by others
    Soon press through our soil of deeds.
The sprouting of compassion
    Draws its light from human needs.

The stand of our humanity
    Extends its slender reach.
The forming buds attest our growth,
    Potential filling each.

And in the spring of giving,
    In the moisture of concern,
The flower lets its dignity
    Unfold, its colors burn.

How often is the ground prepared,
    Examples softly sown,
And flowers fail to blossom,
    Stems of caring scarcely grown?

Yet hallowed is the moment,
    Which in some forever looms,
When love unfolds its canopy
    And, softly helping, blooms.

LOVE ACROSS TIME

Love has one dimension
    That's beyond both time and space.
No amount of living
    Can this vital force erase.

The heart preserves a dialog,
    A unity of spirit,
That taps the beauty of the past
    And keeps you always near it.

You remain the eyes and ears,
    The pulse of one you love.
Thoughts comprise an open dream
    To one you're thinking of.

Two minds that fuse in consciousness
    Become the same as one.
The link that love provides through time
    Can never be undone.

All the things that cross your heart
    And you would like to share
Are telegraphed in spirit
    To the love that's always there.

IT WAS BEAUTIFUL

Living out life's moments
    We've become caring, sharing
        Passengers
Who voyage through time and space,
    Locked together
        In motion
            And tender dreaming.

The quiet beauty
    And casual eloquence
        Of our lives
Brings harmony and warmth
    And shared hope.

Our spirits are nourished
    In those rest places
        Of the mind
Where time slows just enough
    To still confusion
And sharpen perceptions
    Of the heart.

Such impressions link up
    In a love-inspired continuum
To give us that line of resistance
    Against fear, sadness, regret
And to promote compassion
    And caring.

I look now and again
   At past images
      And future impressions
And think how nice it will be
   If my last mortal image,
      Bountiful and complete,
         Powered by an unending love,
Mirrors the present
   And repeats once again —
      "It was beautiful."

THE PATH WE LEAVE BEHIND

We walked the shores together
    Leaving footprints in the sand.
The cleansing action of the waves
    Behind us licked the land.

We dreamed our way across the sand
    As others had before.
We left our new impressions
    Printed softly on the shore.

And when we turned around
    And later walked again that ground,
We looked for traces left before
    But not a trace was found.

We felt the tidal motion
    Moving up and over feet
And sensed that rare and fleeting
    Gift of chance when spirits meet.

We felt the moist reminder
    That our love's a special place
Where hearts inscribe a message
    For the ages to erase.

And clasping lives we moved ahead
    As nature had designed
And covered all the shores we could
    And never looked behind.

ABOUT THE AUTHOR

Bruce B. Wilmer, 46, is from Long Island, New York. He met his wife of 21 years, Sydney, while studying English and history at the University of Rochester. Enrolling in law school following his 1967 graduation, he was drafted after one year due to the Vietnam War. He first began writing light verse for diversion while he was at the Army Intelligence School in Maryland. He married Sydney in 1969 just days before his departure to Bonn, Germany, where he was assigned to the American Embassy. She joined him several months later after concluding her teaching year and spent two years with him in Germany. At the end of his Army tour, they moved to New Hampshire's lake and mountain region, where Bruce worked in real estate finance and recreational development. While in Germany and New Hampshire, Bruce cultivated an intense interest in writing poetry.

In early 1976, a few months after moving back to Long Island, their first child, a son, was born. His early smiles prompted Bruce's poem, *A Baby's Smile*, which was the catalyst in the formation of their business, Wilmer Graphics. Using hand-set lead type and an antiquated letter press purchased at auction, they printed and personalized the poem on parchment. This was the first of hundreds of poetry titles, known as *Light Lines*™ *Originals*, produced over the next fourteen years in the form of scrolls, posters and greeting cards. As time passed, the business expanded into progressively larger quarters, developing more modern printing techniques and catering to a worldwide market. One such relocation occurred simultaneously with the birth of their daughter in 1981.

Bruce feels fortunate that writing poetry, once his spare time obsession, is now his life's work and that he can share feelings of love, friendship, inspiration and understanding with others.